A READ-FROM-BOTH-SIDES COMIC BOOK

CAT JOKES
VS
DOG JOKES

CAT JOKES TOLD BY DOGS: AN EPIC COMEDY BATTLE

WOOF!
Read on for jokes that make dogs howl with laughter!

DAVID LEWMAN
ILLUSTRATED BY **JOHN McNAMEE**

WORKMAN ✿ NEW YORK

ABOUT THE AUTHOR

DAVID LEWMAN is the author of more than 155 books for young readers starring such well-known characters as SpongeBob, Batman, Teenage Mutant Ninja Turtles, Minions, and Trolls. He's also written 71 SpongeBob comics, several of which were chosen by Stephen Hillenburg for his "best of" collections. David has written TV scripts for shows on Nickelodeon, Disney, Netflix, Cartoon Network, Comedy Central, NBC, and MTV, including *Kick Buttowski*, *George of the Jungle*, *Spaceballs: The Animated Series*, *The Unstoppable Yellow Yeti*, *Drawn Together*, and *3rd Rock from the Sun*. He has no pets at the moment but once played Snoopy in *You're a Good Man, Charlie Brown* to rave reviews. David lives in Los Angeles with his wife, Donna.

ABOUT THE ILLUSTRATOR

JOHN McNAMEE is a cartoonist and writer living in Los Angeles. He has contributed to Cartoon Network, the *New Yorker*, *Mad Magazine*, the *Onion News Network*, and Clickhole. He is also the fur-dad to Misty, the sweetest little kitten.

Copyright © 2023 by David Lewman

Illustration copyright © 2023 by John McNamee

All rights reserved. No portion of this book may be reproduced—mechanically, electronically, or by any other means, including photocopying—without written permission of the publisher.

Library of Congress Cataloging-in-Publication Data is available.

ISBN 978-1-5235-1205-8

Design by Daniella Graner and Kara Strubel

Workman books are available at special discounts when purchased in bulk for premiums and sales promotions as well as for fundraising or educational use. Special editions or book excerpts can also be created to specification. For details, please contact special.markets@hbgusa.com.

Workman Publishing Co., Inc., a subsidiary of Hachette Book Group, Inc.
1290 Avenue of the Americas
New York, NY 10104

workman.com

Distributed in Europe by Hachette Livre,
58 rue Jean Bleuzen, 92 178 Vanves Cedex, France.

Distributed in the United Kingdom by Hachette Book Group, UK,
Carmelite House, 50 Victoria Embankment, London EC4Y 0DZ.

WORKMAN is a registered trademark of Workman Publishing Co., Inc.,
a subsidiary of Hachette Book Group, Inc.
Printed in China on responsibly sourced paper.
First printing July 2023
10 9 8 7 6 5 4 3 2 1

CAT JOKES

CAT JOKES

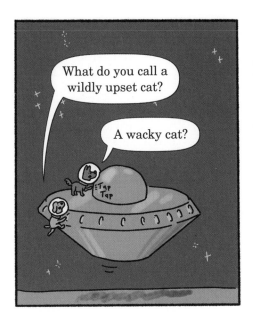

THE SMART DOG'S GUIDE TO LITTLE-KNOWN CATS!

Which cat has a dark face, blue eyes, and long antlers?

THE SIAMOOSE CAT!

Which cat goes great with ice cream?

THE CALICONE CAT!

Which cat has four legs, two eyes, and a roof?

THE HOUSE CAT!

Which cat always carries everything it needs . . . AND MORE?

THE PURSE-IAN CAT!

KNOW YOUR ENEMY

Which cat is allergic to itself?

The Bur-sneeze Cat!

Which cat goes great
with spaghetti?

The Meatball-inese!

What do you get when you cross
a little cat and a rabbit?

The American Short Hare!

Which cat grows
on the floor
of the rain forest?

The Fungal Cat!

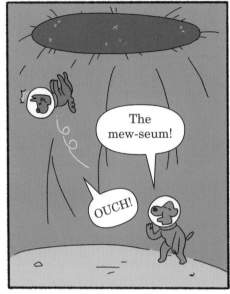

A READ-FROM-BOTH-SIDES COMIC BOOK

DOG JOKES

— VS —

CAT JOKES

DOG JOKES TOLD BY CATS: AN EPIC COMEDY BATTLE

MEOW!
Read on for jokes that make cats yowl with laughter!

DAVID LEWMAN

ILLUSTRATED BY **JOHN McNAMEE**

WORKMAN ❖ NEW YORK

ABOUT THE AUTHOR

DAVID LEWMAN is the author of more than 155 books for young readers starring such well-known characters as SpongeBob, Batman, Teenage Mutant Ninja Turtles, Minions, and Trolls. He's also written 71 SpongeBob comics, several of which were chosen by Stephen Hillenburg for his "best of" collections. David has written TV scripts for shows on Nickelodeon, Disney, Netflix, Cartoon Network, Comedy Central, NBC, and MTV, including *Kick Buttowski*, *George of the Jungle*, *Spaceballs: The Animated Series*, *The Unstoppable Yellow Yeti*, *Drawn Together*, and *3rd Rock from the Sun*. He has no pets at the moment but once played Snoopy in *You're a Good Man, Charlie Brown* to rave reviews. David lives in Los Angeles with his wife, Donna.

ABOUT THE ILLUSTRATOR

JOHN McNAMEE is a cartoonist and writer living in Los Angeles. He has contributed to Cartoon Network, the *New Yorker*, *Mad Magazine*, the *Onion News Network*, and Clickhole. He is also the fur-dad to Misty, the sweetest little kitten.

Library of Congress Cataloging-in-Publication Data is available.

ISBN 978-1-5235-1205-8

Design by Daniella Graner and Kara Strubel

Workman books are available at special discounts when purchased in bulk for premiums and sales promotions as well as for fundraising or educational use. Special editions or book excerpts can also be created to specification. For details, please contact special.markets@hbgusa.com.

Workman Publishing Co., Inc., a subsidiary of Hachette Book Group, Inc.
1290 Avenue of the Americas
New York, NY 10104

workman.com

Distributed in Europe by Hachette Livre,
58 rue Jean Bleuzen, 92 178 Vanves Cedex, France.

Distributed in the United Kingdom by Hachette Book Group, UK,
Carmelite House, 50 Victoria Embankment, London EC4Y 0DZ.

WORKMAN is a registered trademark of Workman Publishing Co., Inc.,
a subsidiary of Hachette Book Group, Inc.
Printed in China on responsibly sourced paper.
First printing July 2023
10 9 8 7 6 5 4 3 2 1

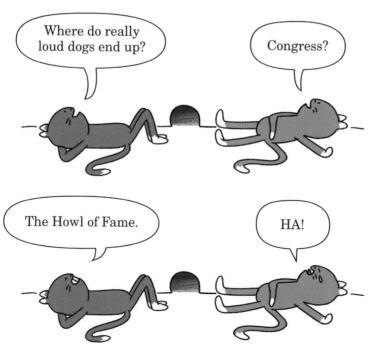

THE SMART CAT'S GUIDE TO LITTLE-KNOWN DOGS!

What kind of dogs do you use in your nose at the pool?

NOSE PUGS!

Which dog is best at kicking a black-and-white ball?

THE SOCCER SPANIEL!

What do you get when you cross a short-legged dog with an electric eel?

A SHOCKS-HUND!

Which kind of dog is green and fuzzy?

THE MOLDIN' RETRIEVER!

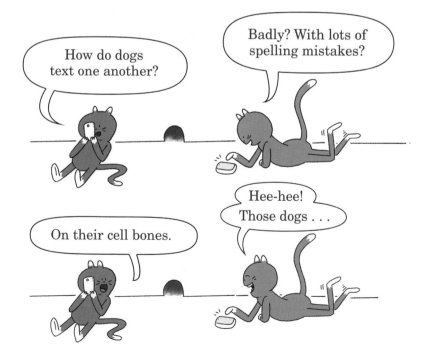

KNOW YOUR ENEMY

Which dog never blows its nose?

THE SNOTWEILER!

Which dog is the nerdiest?

THE LABRADORK RETRIEVER!

Which dog is the best jumper?

THE PIT BULL-FROG!

Which dog tells tales that go on and on and on?

THE NEVERENDING CORGI!

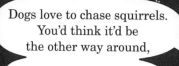

Dogs love to chase squirrels. You'd think it'd be the other way around,

'cause dogs are NUTS!

Why'd the dog try to get adopted by Prince Charming?

He'd heard the prince was always throwing balls!

How many dogs does it take to screw in a light bulb?

Two—one to screw it in and the other to sniff its butt!

I actually don't know if a dog *can* screw in a light bulb,

but I know I'd like to socket!

I once knew a dog who couldn't keep a secret.

He was a BLAB-SOME-MORE Retriever!

Somebody dog-eared the pages of my book. *Now every time the mail comes, the book barks!*

Well, I'd better get out of here—it looks like it's going to rain us and them!

CAT

Ha-ha! But dogs aren't THAT bad, am I right?

What do you call married dogs?

A snappy couple?

Not bad, but I was thinking "husband and woof."

Keep thinking.

Mom! What do you get when you cross dogs and candy?

Uh, dear? Be careful . . .

Sour Pooch Kids!